HANUMAN

As told by

Radhika Sekar

Illustrated & Designed by David Badour
Edited by Sylvia Pollard

Vakils, Feffer & Simons Pvt. Ltd. Mumbai, India

Hanuman
Radhika Sekar
Ottawa, Canada
www.radikhasekar.com

Illustrated & Designed by David Badour
Ottawa, Canada
www.badour.ca

Edited by Pollard Editing
Ottawa, Canada
www.pollardediting.com

Price in India Rs. 195/-

A Kaleidoscope Book

Published by Arun K. Mehta for Vakils, Feffer and Simons Pvt. Ltd.
Industry Manor, Appasaheb Marathe Marg
Prabhadevi, Mumbai 400 025, India

Printed by Bimal A Mehta at Vakils & Sons Pvt. Ltd.
Industry Manor, Appasaheb Marathe Marg
Prabhadevi, Mumbai 400 025, India

Web Site: www.vakilspublications.com
Email: info@vakilspublications.com
Phone: 91-22-24306780
Fax: 91-22-24225111

ISBN.: 978-81-87111-88-7

To
My brother Raghu, a staunch devotee of Lord Hanuman,
And
Grandsons Maverick and Parker — RS

To
Bonnie, for your help and inspiration
And
Daughters Sadie and Naomi — DB

Contents

Birth of Hanuman

Long, long ago, in ancient times, there lived a beautiful *apsara** named Anjana and she lived at the court of the great goddess Parvati.

Anjana was as beautiful as she was mischievous and one day Parvati caught her imitating her.

The goddess was not pleased. "How dare you mimic me like a monkey," cried Parvati. "For this I banish you to live amongst the *vanaras** in *Kishkindha!*"*

Poor Anjana! She fell to her knees and begged forgiveness.

The other apsaras joined in pleading with the goddess not to send Anjana away. Even Vayu, the wind—who secretly loved Anjana—came forward, but to no avail. The goddess Parvati would not be appeased.

Despondent, Anjana packed her belongings and bade farewell to her friends.

Parvati's husband, the great god Shiva, felt sorry for Anjana. "I cannot revoke Parvati's curse," he told her sadly. "But I promise you a heroic son whose fame will spread to the four corners of the world."

---

* *apsara.* celestial nymph
* *vanaras.* mythical tribe, half man/half monkey, with great strength and powers of speech
* *Kishkindha.* land of the vanaras

Thus it came to pass that Anjana settled in Kishkindha. There she married a noble vanara called Kesari and in due time she bore a son.

Half godly and half vanara, the child was as radiant as the great god Shiva himself and also playful like his mother and full of pranks. But he possessed a great deal of charm and his good nature endeared him to everyone.

One day he looked up and saw Surya, the sun, blazing through the sky like a golden ball.

"O, a juicy orange!" he cried, clapping his hands and jumping up and down excitedly. "I must have it."

With a giant leap, he sprang into the sky toward Surya with his hands stretched out.

Surya saw him coming and, startled, lost his balance, sending the stars and planets crashing toward each other.

Indra, Lord of Thunder, who was riding by on his white elephant, dashed to Surya's rescue.

"Halt!" he ordered, in a thunderous voice. Clouds rumbled and lightning flashed as he spoke. Pointing a magical finger, he aimed a thunderbolt that whizzed through the air like lightning, striking the boy in the jaw!

"Ow-w-w … !" cried the boy as he tumbled, tears welling in his eyes. His jaw and feelings were badly hurt. He would have crashed to the ground had Vayu, the wind, not rushed to his aid. Gently sweeping him up in his sinewy arms, he carried the boy to safety.

Vayu was enraged when he saw that the boy's jaw was broken.

"Who would use such force against a helpless child?" he demanded angrily. "Let they who harmed him choke to death."

And in so saying, he began sucking away all the air from the universe.

Panic broke out as gods, devas, asuras, humans, and all the creatures of the world gathered to voice their concern. For without air life is impossible.

"Indra is to blame for this!" they cried. "It was he who harmed the boy, so it is he who should placate Vayu."

"Forgive me, Vayu," begged Indra humbly. "It was wrong of me to use force. To make amends, I grant the child two gifts: the speed of lightning and protection from the elements. Neither fire nor water shall ever harm him."

"We bestow upon him the power to change the size and shape of his body at will," added the asuras, also anxious to appease Vayu.

"And we give him power over the planets, especially *Shani*,"* cried the heavenly bodies.

Even the great god Brahma, Creator of the World, stepped up. "I grant that he will live as long as he wishes and choose the time of his end," he declared.

Pleased with these blessings, Vayu released air back into the universe and the world breathed easily again.

Flowers fell from the sky as the boy rushed into his mother's loving arms.

Vayu looked on indulgently and named him Hanuman—Broken Jaw, declaring: "You will be my son and have the strength of the wind. Your charm and playful spirit will endear you to all and, in time, you will use your gifts to fight tyranny and injustice."

"*Thatha stu!* So be it!" chorused gods, devas, asuras, humans, and all the creatures of the world.

And to this day, Hanuman is hailed as the bravest of the brave, champion of justice, protector against planetary influences, and loved by all for his playful, childlike nature.

* *Shani.* Saturn, who can be both good and vicious

Schooling with Surya

Years passed. Hanuman reached the age* when, in ancient times, boys began their formal education. It was time for him to seek a guru.

"Surya sees everything there is to see and knows everything there is to know," said Hanuman to his mother. "I will, therefore, ask him to be my guru."

But Surya recognized him as the child who had thrown the sky into chaos. "Aren't you the boy who thought I was a fruit?" he asked warily.

"Yes, sir," replied Hanuman sheepishly. "But I was only a child then." Standing up as tall as he could, and with a serious face, he added, "I'm older now, and more sensible."

Surya, however, was too busy to take on a pupil. "From dawn to dusk I ride across the sky. By sunset I am tired and need to rest," he explained. "You must find another guru."

Hanuman, however, was persistent. "Ple-e-e-ase," he pleaded. "I have the speed of lightning and the strength of the wind and could fly alongside your chariot as you ride across the sky."

Impressed by his determination, Surya finally agreed and Hanuman became his pupil.

* eight years

Thereafter, Hanuman flew alongside Surya's chariot, from dawn to dusk, paying close attention to what Surya said. At night, when Surya retired, Hanuman stayed up do his homework. But he was up at dawn, bright and ready to fly alongside his guru's chariot once more.

Hanuman had a quick and curious mind and Surya was very pleased with him. Soon he had taught Hanuman everything that he needed to know.

"Dear one," said Surya. "You have mastered the four books of knowledge, called Vedas, and the six philosophies, called Darshanas. You excel at all sixty-four arts and understand the one hundred eight supernatural mysteries of the world. You are well versed in literature, politics, diplomacy, commerce, yoga, martial arts, music, and the sciences. Besides all this, you are also sweet-natured and modest and have grown into a well-rounded young man of whom I am proud. Your education is complete and it is now time for you to go out into the world."

Hanuman was excited. But he was also sad for he would now have to part from his guru. Bowing low, he addressed Surya with reverence: "O Wise Master, I am ever grateful for the knowledge you have given me. Now it is time to show my gratitude.* Ask of me anything and it shall be yours."

"Dear boy, watching you study was a great delight and reward enough for me," replied Surya solemnly. "However, if you insist, I ask that you look after the welfare of my son Sugriva, who, like you, is a vanara."

"*Thatha stu!* So be it!" declared Hanuman.

After blessing his pupil and wishing him good fortune, Surya embraced Hanuman and they parted ways.

* it is customary for pupils to honour their gurus with a *dakshina*, a gift, when their education is completed

Sugriva & Wicked King Vaali

Surya's son Sugriva, like Hanuman, was a vanara, and he and his troop*
lived in the dense forests of Kishkindha. His stepbrother, Vaali, was
their leader.

Now Vaali was a very selfish king and ruled by jungle law, which
permits the strong to dominate the weak. He kept the best fruit trees for
himself and bullied his subjects, constantly making them serve him like
slaves. They were all terrified of him.

One day, a fierce rakshasa appeared at their grove. Laughing wickedly,
he seized their fruits and demanded that they gather him more.

Furious, Vaali bared his teeth and, beating his chest threateningly,
stood up to fight him. Not expecting to be challenged, the rakshasa—who
was really quite cowardly—started to run away. But Vaali, who loved
fighting, chased after him.

With Vaali close at his heels, the rakshasa ran through the grove and
through the forest until he reached the hills. Further into the hills he went
until at last he came to a cave in a particularly remote hillside and ran into
it to hide. But Vaali, unfazed, continued to follow him.

* monkeys live in troops

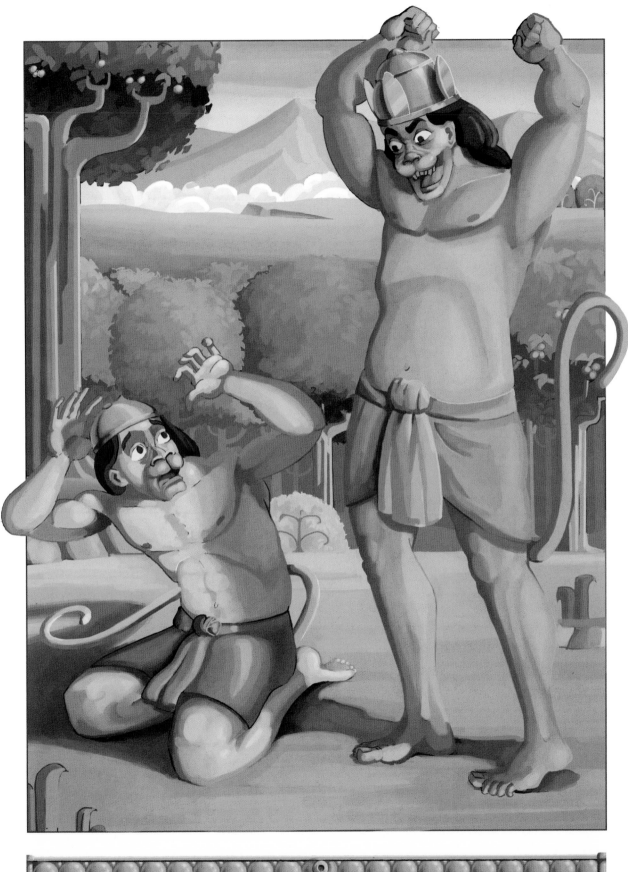

Hours passed. Sugriva and the others waited outside. They heard sounds of a fierce battle raging inside. Then there was a sudden blood-curdling scream, a thud, followed by silence. The fight had ended.

But who had won?

The vanaras listened anxiously for Vaali's cry of triumph. When they heard nothing, they thought that the rakshasa had killed Vaali. Fearing that he would now attack them, they rolled a huge boulder to the mouth of the cave, sealed it, and returned to Kishkindha.

But Vaali had not been defeated. In fact, he had killed the rakshasa but had been too exhausted to call out. After resting a while to catch his breath, he made his way to the mouth of the cave. Imagine his shock when he found a huge boulder blocking the exit!

Gathering his strength, he heaved and pushed until the boulder rolled away. Crawling out, he gradually made his way back to Kishkindha.

There, expecting a hero's welcome, Vaali found instead that Sugriva had been declared king! Not only was he sitting on Vaali's throne, he was also wearing his crown!

Enraged, Vaali set upon his stepbrother. "Traitor!" he roared. "You left me to die in the cave so that you could steal my throne?"

Sugriva tried to explain that they had all thought Vaali was dead. But Vaali was in no mood to listen. He pummelled him with blows until a bruised and bloodied Sugriva ran for his life. But Vaali chased after him. "I will chase you to the ends of the world and then I'll kill you!"

Poor Sugriva! Panting, he fled through the forest, past valleys and streams, meadows and woods, until at last he came to a mountainside *ashram** on the banks of the sacred river Pampa.

"Help me, please!" Sugriva called out to the sage who lived there. "Vaali is after my life."

Now, long ago, Vaali had misbehaved and angered this very sage, who had warned him never to set foot in his ashram or his head would burst into a thousand pieces. Opening the gates, the sage invited Sugriva in, saying, "Vaali will not dare come here. You will be quite safe."

* *ashram.* a sage's retreat

Vaali stopped in his tracks when he saw that Sugriva had taken refuge with the sage. Seething with rage, he returned to Kishkindha and punished his subjects for declaring Sugriva their king. Still not satisfied, he took up position outside the ashram from where he taunted Sugriva night and day.

"Coward," he jeered, beating his chest and gnashing his teeth. "Your family members are now my slaves. What do you think of that?"

To harass him further, Vaali began swooping down from overhead—being careful not to set foot in the sage's ashram—and whacking Sugriva on the head.

It was around this time that Hanuman appeared looking for Sugriva. Finding him in such a pitiful state, he decided to help him.

"Your father, Surya, asked me to look out for your welfare," said Hanuman, feeling sorry for Sugriva, "therefore, I will stop Vaali from harassing you."

The next time Vaali flew overhead, Hanuman caught hold of his feet.

Surprised, Vaali looked down and recognized Hanuman with some apprehension. He was well aware of Hanuman's strength and skill.

If this vanara manages to drag me down to the ground, my head will burst into a thousand pieces, thought Vaali anxiously. I must get away.

Wriggling and twisting, he tried to free himself from Hanuman's grip. But Hanuman was strong and held on tightly. Vaali tried to fly higher, but Hanuman pulled him lower again. And so they struggled for some time.

At last Hanuman said, "I will let go if you promise not to harm Sugriva."

Vaali, who was getting tired, agreed readily. "But he must not return to Kishkindha," he warned, "or I will certainly kill him."

The Two Fine Princes of Ayodhya

Although Vaali had promised not to hurt him, Sugriva, nevertheless, feared leaving the safety of the sage's ashram. He, therefore, decided to make his home on a small hill close by. He was soon joined by other vanaras who preferred exile to living under Vaali's rule.

"Vaali is a tyrant," they grumbled. "He keeps the best trees for himself and bullies us mercilessly. Good rulers are always kind to their subjects and share their wealth."

"If I were king, I would share all I had," replied Sugriva. The monkeys cheered and made him their leader.

The years passed uneventfully until, one day, while Hanuman was roaming on the banks of the river Pampa, he saw a golden chariot flying in the sky. It was drawn by five green-horned mules and driven by a ten-headed rakshasa who was laughing maliciously. By his side cowered a beautiful woman, crying piteously. As they flew by, she furtively removed a bracelet from her wrist and cast it over the side of the chariot.

Rushing to the spot where the bracelet fell, Hanuman saw that it was made of gold and studded with precious gems. This can only belong to a princess, he thought. But who?

A few days later, Hanuman was sitting in a mango tree enjoying its sweet, golden fruit when he heard voices from below.

Peeping through the branches, he saw two handsome strangers. They were dressed as woodsmen but had a royal air about them. And they were both sad.

The older youth wrung his hands and repeated, "We must find her and rescue her."

"But how?" inquired the other. "Ravana is all-powerful and has a large army of gruesome rakshasas. Also, Lord Brahma's boon has made him mightier than any deva or asura. We are merely men and have neither his magic powers nor their colossal strength. How can we fight him?"

"We must, at least, try," said the first youth. "Poor Sita will be so sad and frightened."

Could they be talking about the beautiful princess that I saw in the flying chariot? wondered Hanuman.

He leapt down from the branch and faced them. "Who are you fine strangers? And why are you so sad?" he asked.

Startled, the youths unsheathed their daggers—ready to defend themselves. But when they saw that this vanara was unarmed they relaxed.

"We are princes of Ayodhya," explained the dark youth. "I am Rama and this is my brother Lakshmana."

Rama then explained how his stepmother had banished him to the forest for twelve years so that her own son could reign as king. His wife, the beautiful princess Sita, and brother Lakshmana, from whom he was inseparable, had accompanied him into exile.

"We were very happy living in the forest until Sita was abducted by the ten-headed rakshasa, Ravana," said Rama, tears welling in his eyes.

"Is this hers?" asked Hanuman, showing him the bracelet that the beautiful woman had dropped from the flying chariot. Rama recognized it at once. Hanuman then explained how he came to have it.

"We are on our way to Ravana's kingdom to rescue Sita," explained Lakshmana. "But alas, we have no army. How can we fight the mighty Ravana?"

"Perhaps I can help," suggested Hanuman. "But first you must meet my friends."

Using the powers that the asuras had granted him, Hanuman took a big breath. His body swelled and grew until he became a giant. Then, placing the princes on either shoulder, he flew back with them to the camp on the hill near the sage's ashram.

Sugriva and the others crowded around them curiously. They had never seen such noble humans before. Rama, once again, recounted his sad story, this time to Sugriva and the monkeys.

"But why did you not take the kingdom by force?" asked Sugriva, puzzled by Rama's explanation of how he came to be exiled.

"My father gave his word and I intend to honour it," said Rama solemnly.

"Why must you rescue Sita?" asked one of the monkeys. "Surely there are many other beautiful women who could replace her?"

"Sita is my wife," responded Rama with feeling. "I love her dearly and promised to protect and cherish her always. Besides, she was taken against her will and it is my duty as a warrior to fight cruelty and injustice. The strong must always protect the helpless from bullies."

So far, the monkeys had only experienced jungle law. So Rama's words were new and strange to them. Sugriva then told the princes how Vaali had chased him out of Kishkindha without hearing him out. "He is a tyrant!"

One by one, the vanaras came forward to tell of their problems with Vaali.

"He treated me like a slave," said one.

"He seized all of my mangoes," said another.

"He beat me if I disobeyed him," said yet another.

"Exile in the forest is better than living under his rule," they all agreed.

"Bullies like Vaali have no right to rule," pronounced Rama on hearing their tales of woe.

"Can you help us get rid of him?" asked Sugriva with hope. "If you do, we will help you rescue your Sita."

"A monkey army to fight Ravana?" scoffed Lakshmana, amused.

But Rama silenced his brother with a frown. "No effort is too small," he said. "We have justice on our side ... and goodness always triumphs in the end."

Thus, Rama agreed to help the vanaras overthrow the wicked Vaali. In return they agreed to help him against Ravana.

It was decided that Sugriva should first try reasoning with Vaali to let him form his own troop.

"But he will come after me when he sees me," protested Sugriva anxiously.

"I will intervene if he attacks," promised Rama.

The monkeys and princes then marched to Kishkindha.

"Vaali, dear brother," called Sugriva. "May we talk?"

But no sooner had Vaali seen Sugriva than he grabbed him roughly by the neck. "I warned you never to return here. Now I will have to kill you," he cried and began pounding poor Sugriva.

Sugriva was no match for Vaali; bruised and bleeding, he soon fell to the ground. Vaali would have leapt upon him and killed him had Rama not stepped forward, bow in hand.

"Stop!" he called with authority. But Vaali was too involved with beating Sugriva to hear. Therefore, the prince released an arrow from his bow, which whizzed through the air and found its mark in Vaali's wicked heart!

Falling to the ground, Vaali growled at Rama, "This was not your business. You had no right to interfere."

"Oh, but it was and it will continue to be," replied Rama coldly. "I have vowed to defend the weak from bullies like you."

Sugriva and his friends cheered as Vaali gasped and spluttered. But the prince ran up to the fallen vanara and knelt beside him.

"You were strong and brave and would have been a good king. But greed and pride made you a tyrant and led to your downfall."

Cradling Vaali's head in his arms, Rama said gently, "May peace be upon you, my friend."

The anger and harshness left Vaali's face as serenity descended upon him. Smiling up at Rama, he closed his eyes for the last time.

The Monsoon Season

With Vaali's defeat, Sugriva was hailed as the new king of the troop. Everyone was happy to see the end of Vaali's tyranny. True to his word, Sugriva shared his wealth with his subjects and introduced laws to protect women, children, and the weak.

Soon thereafter, the monsoons began and the vanaras took to the trees for cover. Rama and his brother Lakshmana found shelter in a nearby cave.

Hanuman, fascinated by the young princes, stayed with them in the cave. There, huddled together as the rain fell in torrents, they talked about ethics and moral behaviour. Rama explained to Hanuman that life depends on how you handle everyday matters.

"All actions, even the seemingly unimportant ones, have a bearing on our future," he said. "Therefore, always think carefully before acting. You reap what you sow—that is the law of karma."

Rama then described the five sacred principles that one should cultivate: "Non-violence, faithfulness, honesty, moderation, and truth.

"Non-violence," he went on to explain, "of word, thought, and deed. For there is no point thinking violent thoughts while pretending to be peaceful. That's hypocrisy!

"Faithfulness is being true to those around you …

"Honesty is not stealing or lying …

"Moderation is maintaining balance in all things. The greatest problems are created by greed and extremes in behaviour, as these are harmful to body, mind, and spirit …

"Above all else is truth. For only truth can set you free!"

Hanuman was awed by the prince's words. But he was also puzzled. "Forgive me, dear Prince," he began hesitantly, "how can warriors practice non-violence? Aren't they required to kill their enemies?"

The princes smiled knowingly for this had puzzled them too.

"Listen carefully," said Rama, drawing Hanuman closer. "The law of Nature combines both life and death. Rain creates food, food is eaten by all beings, and they, in turn, may feed upon other beings. Killing for revenge or greed has no place in this cycle. A true warrior hates injustice and raises a sword only to protect others. A true warrior feels no anger towards an enemy, feeling only compassion for those who act violently, understanding that they do so because they don't know better."

"Is this why you so lovingly comforted Vaali?" asked Hanuman.

"Yes," replied the prince. "Everyone is born with the seeds of goodness. In some they take root and bloom into virtues, while in others they remain unripe and buried deep. Vaali had the makings of a great king and warrior. But he was drawn to greed and pride, which held back his true nature."

Inspired by the prince's explanation, Hanuman declared solemnly: "Hereafter I will live by these five principles and dedicate my life to justice and protecting the weak."

Impressed by Hanuman's solemnity, Rama and Lakshmana embraced him. "*Thatha stu!* So be it," they said. "From now on you are our brother in arms."

The Search for Sita

After a week and two months, the monsoons finally withdrew and the vanaras came out of their shelters. They gathered with the princes to discuss Sita's rescue and it was decided that the princes would stay back to train the monkeys in combat. Meanwhile Hanuman was to lead a search party to find Sita.

Before he left, Rama gave Hanuman his ring, saying, "When you find my beloved Sita, give her this ring so that she will know I sent you."

Hanuman and his party travelled south for many days. They crossed mountains, and passed through valleys and dense forests. Along the way they met animals, birds, serpents, and other creatures. Many had seen Ravana's flying chariot and were able to point the way he had taken. Hanuman's friend Jambavan, the King of Bears, also joined them.

At last they came to the coast on the southernmost tip of *Jambudvipa*,* where land meets ocean, and a beautiful water nymph pointed to Ravana's kingdom—the island of Lanka—that lay far beyond.

The vanaras wondered how they could make their way across hundreds of miles of ocean.

---

* *Jambudvipa*. the island of the jambu trees (rose-apple trees); the name is derived from the jambu trees that populated it; it was the ancient name for the Indian subcontinent

"It's too far to jump across," they pointed out, "and we cannot swim, and we don't have a boat."

"The asuras gave me the power to change my form at will," replied Hanuman. "I shall, therefore, make myself as huge as I can and fly across the ocean."

Flexing his muscles, Hanuman took a big breath. Air filled his lungs and his body throbbed with energy as he grew bigger … and bigger … and still bigger. At last he was taller than a coconut tree. His eyes blazing like comets, his fists clenched, his hands stretched wide, he sprang into the sky.

Clouds parted to make way for Vayu's son. Stars shone brightly to light his way. Fish, turtles, whales, and other creatures of the sea rose to the surface to watch him as he flew across their ocean. Hanuman looked down and waved to them as he passed above.

Halfway across the ocean, the waters turned dark and stormy. There was wild thrashing and swirling. Suddenly—from out of the depths—a long, hooded head loomed into the air, hissing and swishing and shrieking, "Who dares cross this ocean?"

It was Surasa, the mother of serpents, and it had been ordained that no one could cross the southern seas without entering her mouth. So far, no creature had ever managed to pass her for she swallowed everyone whole.

Hanuman realized he would have to enter her mouth in order to cross the ocean. He took a deep breath and swelled his body with air as Surasa opened her mouth wide to accommodate him. Hanuman took another breath and his body grew larger. Another, and grew larger, and Surasa opened wider … then wider … until her mouth was stretched to the limit.

Suddenly Hanuman exhaled and the air came whooshing out as he shrank to the size of a bee! He then zoomed into the serpent's mouth and—in the blink of an eye—zipped out again before Surasa could close her mouth to swallow him!

"There! I have passed through your mouth. Now, let me pass," demanded Hanuman triumphantly. Realizing that she had been outwitted, Surasa had to let him go.

With a chuckle, Hanuman flew on.

Soon he saw a glittering haze on the horizon. He had arrived on the island of Lanka.

As he came near, he saw gleaming citadels of gold, with graceful arches and gem-studded doors. Even the city's ramparts were ornately covered in precious stones and filigreed engravings. Bright red flags fluttered from every tower. What a splendour to behold!

It was dawn when Hanuman landed and the rakshasas—who sleep by day and wake at night—had just retired to bed.

Only Lankini, the guardian spirit, stomped about outside the walls, for she never slept. Spotting Hanuman, she bore down on him, her eyes blazing fiercely. "Halt! Who goes there?" she challenged.

Impatient to pass through the gates, Hanuman, once again, swelled into a giant. Head in the stars and tail lashing the ocean into gigantic waves, he let out a piercing scream.

Terrified, Lankini dropped her weapons and ran away, leaving the gates of Lanka unguarded.

Shrinking to the size of a bee once more, Hanuman flew into Lanka. Undetected, he flew along tree-lined avenues, well-lit squares, golden mansions, and perfumed groves.

Ravana's palace was at the centre of the city. Its golden pillars and crystal floors glistened in the sun.

At the far end of the palace gardens, Hanuman saw a walled garden. An *ashoka** tree stood in the middle of it, under which sat a beautiful woman, guarded on all sides by gruesome rakshasas.

They were taunting her: "Your husband is not coming," they sniggered. "He must have found someone else already."

"Why would anyone want you?" jeered another, rudely prodding the woman in the ribs. "You are such a skinny little thing."

"Give in to Ravana or he'll eat you alive," threatened a third.

---

* *ashoka*. this tree—botanical name *Saraca indica*—is considered sacred in India; meaning "absence of sorrow," it is a very handsome, erect evergreen with deep green foliage and fragrant orange flowers that turn red; in bloom between April and May

Although the woman under the tree was forlorn, there was great dignity in her bearing. She did not react to the taunts but merely closed her eyes in meditation.

Hanuman knew at once that he had found the princess, Sita.

Changing back to normal size, he perched on a branch above her, awaiting an opportunity to speak to her.

Soon the rakshasas grew tired of jeering Sita. The sun had risen to its highest point. Drowsy, they laid down to sleep.

Waiting until he heard their snores, Hanuman dropped Rama's ring into Sita's lap.

With a gasp of recognition, Sita picked up the ring and looked up expectantly. But when she saw Hanuman peering down at her from the branches, she drew back in alarm. Placing a finger on his lips, Hanuman beckoned her to be quiet lest she awaken the guards.

"Sh-h-h ... I am Hanuman, son of Vayu," he whispered. "Rama sent me to tell you that he is on his way to rescue you."

A smile lit up Sita's face. "I knew he would come," she said.

"If you climb onto my back, I could carry you back with me," offered Hanuman.

But Sita declined his offer. "No," she said. "Ravana must be confronted or he will not stop bullying people. Tell my lord that I await his arrival with patience."

Sita then gave him a jewelled hairpin to give to Rama as proof of their meeting.

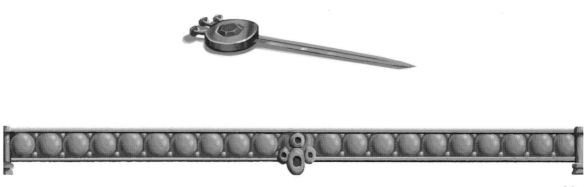

The Burning of Lanka

His mission complete, Hanuman bade Sita farewell. But he decided to have some fun before flying back.

Springing to the ground, he shrieked to awaken the rakshasas from their slumber.

Lazily they stirred and, looking up, dully saw a monkey flailing about.

"Go away," they grumbled, but Hanuman only lunged at them, chattering louder than ever. He would not let them go back to sleep no matter how much they hissed and tried to chase him away. Irritated and now wide awake, they decided to capture him. But Hanuman was too quick and ran circles around them. He pulled their dishevelled braids, and mimicked their shrieks.

What an uproar!

Hearing the commotion, the royal guards arrived to investigate. But they, too, were no match for the nimble Hanuman. Taunting them, Hanuman leapt over their heads when cornered and escaped their grasp.

The sun was setting as sounds of the racket reached the ears of Ravana, the King of Lanka, who was arising from his sleep. "Capture that pesky ape and bring him to me!" he roared.

They threw nets over Hanuman, but he easily slipped through them.

At last, Ravana's eldest son, Indrajit, who was the most powerful warrior in Lanka, joined the skirmish. Exasperated by the monkey-man's antics, he unleashed his most deadly weapon—the *brahmastra*—an arrow that holds the energy of Lord Brahma!

Too powerful and swift, even for Hanuman, it knocked the wind out of the poor vanara, felling him to the ground. Indrajit then constrained him with serpent ropes and dragged him to his father.

When Hanuman regained awareness, he found himself in Ravana's great hall surrounded by gruesome rakshasas. Although his hands and feet were bound, he managed to shuffle to his feet and stand tall.

"I am Hanuman, son of Vayu, and an envoy of Prince Rama," he declared proudly to Ravana.

At the mention of Rama's name, a hush fell over the court.

"You are no messenger," hissed Ravana spitefully. "You are a silly monkey-man."

"Nonetheless, I am Prince Rama's ambassador. Untie these ropes and offer me a seat, as protocol demands," insisted Hanuman.

"A cage in the royal zoo would suit you better," jeered Ravana, adding, "Is the prince of Ayodhya so desperate that he sends a vanara to speak for him?"

The rakshasas all roared with laughter.

Since he was not offered a chair, Hanuman decided to make a seat for himself. Puffing out his chest, he broke the serpent ropes that had restrained him. Then, lengthening his tail, he coiled it round into a tall stack—taller by half than Ravana's throne—and, leaping upon it, sat down.

The rakshasas were astounded at this feat and drew back warily. "This is no ordinary monkey," they whispered. Even Ravana felt a twinge of alarm.

"Prince Rama is coming with a large army to rescue Sita," said Hanuman. "But if you let her go now, he will not harm you."

"What?!" roared Ravana. "Am I to fear an army of monkeys?"

But Ravana's younger brother, Vibhishana, who did not approve of Ravana's deeds, warned him to be cautious. "This is no ordinary vanara," he said. "He is Hanuman, the son of Vayu, the wind. Heed his words and send Sita back. Make peace with Rama or else we are all doomed."

"Silence!" roared Ravana, enraged. "Lord Brahma granted me power over devas and asuras. How can a mere human with a band of monkeys cause my doom? As for this—this Hanuman creature ... I'll show you what we do to monkey-men."

Ravana called his guards and ordered them to set fire to Hanuman's tail.

It took twenty strong rakshasas to pin Hanuman to the ground. They wrapped an oil-soaked rag to his tail, and set it alight. Then they stood back excitedly to watch him squirm.

But Lord Indra had promised Hanuman immunity from fire. Pushing away the guards, he leapt onto a chandelier. Swinging his long tail, he set fire to the drapes that hung around Ravana's throne. The fire spread and soon the whole court was ablaze. Frothing with fury, Ravana shouted orders as rakshasas ran here and there, some trying to put out the fire while others chased Hanuman in the hope of capturing him before he did further damage.

With a chuckle, Hanuman flew out of the palace and leapt onto the roof. Leaping from roof to roof, he set fire to other buildings. Soon, most of the mansions and pavilions of Lanka were blazing. Golden pillars melted and crumbled, and rakshasas ran into the streets screaming and shouting for water. Children began to cry, and the horses and elephants in the stables went wild. There was pandemonium everywhere. The only spot that Hanuman left untouched was the walled garden where Sita was held.

His task complete, Hanuman leapt into the sky to begin his return journey.

From his palace turret, Ravana saw him flying away and shook his fist in rage.

The Bridge

When Hanuman returned to Kishkindha, he described his visit to Lanka in great detail. To allay Rama's anxiety, promptly he began with his encounter with Sita, presenting him with her jewel-studded hairpin. Then he told them about his adventures in the city.

The vanaras listened in awe as he described the golden city, with its grand mansions and fluttering turrets. They whooped with delight when he told them how he teased the rakshasas and set fire to the city. "Hanuman *ki jai!* Victory to Hanuman!" they shouted, jumping up and down excitedly.

Prince Rama did not approve of Hanuman's antics. "Setting fire to the city was unnecessary," he rebuked. "One must always respect the property of others, even that of our enemies. And what if the children had been hurt?"

Nevertheless, he and Lakshmana joined the victory celebrations. That night they were treated to a sumptuous feast. Baskets of fruit and cups of honey were passed around as Hanuman retold his exploits to the eager vanaras, over and over again, all night long.

The next morning they held a council to prepare for battle. Led by Hanuman, the army followed the princes to the coast. Jambavan joined them with his army of bears.

As they gazed across the vast ocean, they spied a rakshasa heading their way. Lakshmana picked up his bow and arrows, crying, "I will shoot him down!"

But Hanuman recognized the rakshasa. "It is Vibhishana, Ravana's brother," he said. "He disapproves of Ravana's ways and I think he comes to join us."

"He may prove a useful ally," commented Lakshmana, putting down his bow. "But can we trust a person who goes against his brother?"

"Although I love my brother dearly, I disapprove of his wickedness," declared Vibhishana. "I come to fight injustice."

Impressed by his sense of right from wrong, Rama accepted him as an ally.

The princes wondered how they and the vanara army would cross the ocean. They could not fly like Hanuman, nor could they swim. Furthermore, there weren't enough trees to build rafts for all of them.

Rama knelt to the ground and invoked the help of Varuna, the Lord of the Sea. Varuna appeared and suggested that they build a bridge. "I will see that it stays afloat," he promised.

Rama then ordered his troops to build a bridge with the stones and rocks that they found on the seashore. One by one, the vanaras and bears began hurling stones into the ocean under the watchful supervision of Hanuman. Soon, all the creatures of the forest joined in, and vanaras, bears, deer, birds, even little chipmunks, worked side by side with great enthusiasm. The fish, snakes, seals, and other creatures of the sea held the stones together and the bridge to Lanka took shape.

When the bridge was completed, the princes blew their conches and invoked the blessings of Durga, the Goddess of War. Then, beating his chest, Hanuman let out a mighty war cry that filled the heart of every vanara with confidence.

"On to Lanka!" he cried, marching across the bridge.

"On to Lanka!" they chorused, following him.

As they approached, Ravana, who had been watching them carefully all along, ordered his rakshasas to cut the mighty ropes that moored the bridge to the shore of their island.

Unmoored, the bridge floated away and the vanaras' passage was abruptly stopped.

Hanuman went into action. Growing big again, he grabbed the shores of Lanka and stretched himself over the gap. The army scrambled over his back and landed safely on the beach.

The city that Hanuman had burnt down had already been rebuilt and the monkeys and bears gaped in awe at its splendour. "They must possess magic to have restored it so quickly," said Jambavan nervously.

Then, growling menacingly, Hanuman's army marched toward the city's walls. Their voices filled the air and frightened the residents of Lanka.

"Give up Sita and make peace!" they urged.

But Ravana was in no mood to listen. "They are monkeys and bears," he scoffed. "We will chop off their tails and send them scurrying back to the jungle. Come, gather your weapons and fight. Let us drive Rama's rabble away!"

Bugles sounded as the great gates of Lanka slowly opened. Hundreds of rakshasas rushed out, howling and screeching as they advanced. But the monkeys and bears stood firm. Hanuman picked up a stone and hurled it at the rakshasas and the battle began.

Ravana watched from the ramparts as bears startled his army's horses, and monkeys leapt onto their chariots, kicking, punching, scratching, and biting.

Soon the battlefield was enveloped in dust.

The air was filled with the clamour and the clatter of weapons.

Banners were torn, chariots were smashed, and weapons were broken as soldiers on both sides, monkeys and rakshasas, fell wounded to the ground!

Bringing the Magic Herb to Lakshmana

The battle raged on through the day and night. Finally, on the second day, Lakshmana challenged Ravana's son, Indrajit, to combat. They were evenly matched and fought long and hard.

At last, as the sun set, Indrajit decided, once more, to use his deadly weapon—the brahmastra—which holds the energy of the great god Brahma. Dipping it in poison, he hurled it at Lakshmana. Too swift and powerful for the prince to withstand, it knocked Lakshmana to the ground. As the poison coursed through his veins, the prince turned blue and fainted.

A hush fell over the battlefield! Rama, Hanuman, and all of the monkeys gathered around Lakshmana. Even the rakshasas paused to watch.

Jambavan, the bear, picked Lakshmana up tenderly in his arms and carried him to safety. Grief-stricken, Rama cried out, "My poor brother!"

Vibhishana—brother of Ravana—suggested that they fetch Sushena, a skilled rakshasa physician from Lanka.

"But will he help Ravana's enemy?" asked Hanuman.

"He is a doctor," replied Vibhishana, "and does not discriminate between his patients."

Hanuman shrank to the size of a bee once more and flew into Lanka to fetch the doctor and returned with him.

"The poison is spreading rapidly," said the doctor gravely after examining the wounded prince. "Only a special herb called *sanjivini*—which grows far away in the Himalayas—can cure him. Fetch it before sunrise and I will save the prince's life."

With lightning speed, Hanuman set off, flying north across the ocean, past Kishkindha, past the sage's ashram, past sacred rivers, and over the tall Vindhya Mountains that divide the subcontinent in half. He raced through the Ganges valley. Then, at last, he arrived at the Himalayas.

While looking for the herb, Hanuman met a sage who asked him what he was doing. "I'm looking for a special herb that can cure poison. Do you know where I can find it?" Hanuman replied.

Indeed, the sage knew of it. "But it is a holy herb and you must not touch it with unwashed hands. First, wash your hands in that lake and I will help you find it."

Hanuman went to the lake to do as the sage instructed.

But no sooner had he stepped into the lake than a huge crocodile crept up and swallowed him whole! Instantly, Hanuman knew what to do. Puffing out his chest, he grew in size ... larger and larger ... until he was so large that he burst out of the crocodile's belly!

But, to his surprise, not only did the crocodile burst, she had also turned into a beautiful water nymph. "You have liberated me from a curse," she said gratefully. "Now I must warn you: Beware of the sage who directed you here. He is really a rakshasa in disguise and has been ordered by Ravana to stop you, at any cost, from finding the herb you seek. He deliberately sent you to this lake thinking I would swallow you."

Hanuman thanked the nymph and began searching for the herb, taking care to avoid the sage. But he was no botanist and could not tell the plants apart.

Time was running out as the moon was rapidly slipping into the horizon. "Hurry, Hanuman! Very soon it will be time for me to rise again," Surya, the sun, called out anxiously.

Unsure of which herb was the one, Hanuman decided that the only thing for him to do was to carry the whole mountain back to Lanka! Expanding his chest once again, he grew and grew and grew ... until his head reached the sky and his feet went down deep into the underworld. Then, uprooting the mountain with a mighty heave and holding it high above his head, he began his flight back.

Devas, asuras, humans, birds, and all the creatures of the land came out to watch in amazement as Hanuman flew across the sky carrying the mountain! "There goes the son of Vayu!" they cried.

The monkeys cheered as Hanuman placed the mountain in a clearing near the seashore. The doctor quickly found the herb he needed. Grinding it into a paste, he smeared it over Lakshmana's body. They all waited with bated breath.

Just as Chandra, the moon, dipped below the horizon, Lakshmana's eyelids flickered slightly. As Surya's rays filled the earth with light, Lakshmana moved his limbs and sat up! The potion had worked its cure!

There were cheers of joy as Lakshmana jumped up and called for his weapons. He had fully regained his strength and was ready to go back into battle.

Ravana & the Secret Garden

As the battle resumed, Ravana finally entered the fray. Riding in his golden chariot drawn by the five green-horned mules, beating his chest, and shaking his ten heads threateningly, he gave a mighty roar. He was a scary sight!

"Have you come to fight me, Rama?" he mocked with a wicked laugh. "Don't you know that neither deva nor asura can overpower me? Do you think a mere man and a handful of monkeys will succeed?"

But Rama stood his ground fearlessly. Stringing his bow, he let fly ten arrows in quick succession. Whizzing through the air like lightning, they severed Ravana's heads.

However, no sooner did the heads fall to the ground than other heads grew to replace them! Rama released more arrows … and then more … and more! But, each time the heads were severed, others grew back.

Ravana's mocking laughter grew so loud that it shook the earth and rent the sky. "Ha, ha, ha! Is this all you can do?"

Frustrated, Rama sought Vibhishana's advice.

"It is rumoured that Ravana gains his strength from the lotuses that grow in a secret garden," explained Vibhishana. "A few drops of amrita—the elixir of immortality—fell onto the plants there, and, as a result, their flowers induce the power of rejuvenation. They heal even the most lethal wounds.

Ravana eats these lotuses every day, thus his heads grow back as soon as they are chopped off."

Hanuman decided to find the whereabouts of this secret garden. Shrinking to the size of a bee, he planned to stay close to Ravana.

Sure enough, that day, when all had retired, Ravana stole away to some secret destination. Hanuman followed him like a shadow and watched as the rakshasa came to a high wall covered in ivy. Hidden behind the ivy was a gate that led into a garden. Before Ravana could even unlock the gate, Hanuman flew over the wall and entered the now not-so-secret garden.

There he saw a pond filled with lotuses. Still unsighted by Ravana, he very quickly plucked all the flowers, carefully placing them in his knapsack, for surely, he thought, they would be handy later on. Then he drank all the water in the pond and filled it up with silt before flying back to camp.

Ravana fell into a rage when he saw that all the flowers were gone and the pond had been filled in. "This must be that monkey's doing!" he yelled, stamping his feet. "I'll teach him!"

Deprived of his flowers, Ravana was no longer indestructible. Once more his people—and this time even his queen—begged Ravana to make peace.

But the rakshasa was more determined than ever. Mounting his chariot, he charged into battle again. Devas assembled in the sky to watch what was, in all likelihood, to be the final battle between the mighty Ravana and valiant Prince Rama.

The fight was fierce and long. Ravana hurled missiles and wielded his mace, striking down vanaras and bears. Rama tried to stop him but his arrows no more than pierced the rakshasa's tough hide.

Finally Vibhishana whispered to Rama. "Aim for his throat," he said. "That is his most vulnerable spot."

With lightning speed, Rama's arrow sped through the air and found its mark.

"A-H-U-G-G-G-O-O-O-O-H!" roared the mighty Ravana. His scream rent the sky as he fell to the ground with a thud. Ravana was defeated!

Seeing their leader fall, the rakshasa army fled in panic.

The vanaras cheered as they realized that the battle was over. Flowers fell from the sky as devas gathered to rejoice. "It took a man and an army of monkeys and bears to defeat the mighty Ravana!" they chorused.

Hanuman flew into Lanka and informed Sita of Rama's victory. There was great rejoicing as Rama and Sita were reunited.

Bringing out the lotuses that he had carefully stored in his knapsack, Hanuman used them to heal the wounded: monkeys, bears, and even enemy rakshasas—for Rama ordered that they, too, be healed. And soon all jumped up as strong as ever.

"Our period of exile is over," reminded Lakshmana. "We may now return home to Ayodhya."

Kubera, the Lord of Riches, offered them his flying chariot to fly them home.

"How can I thank you for your help?" Rama asked Hanuman.

"My lord," said Hanuman bowing low. "Everything I did was out of friendship and love. I need no praise or reward. All I ask is that I be allowed to spend the rest of my days in your service."

"*Thatha stu!* So be it!" declared Rama, and Hanuman boarded the flying chariot.

Sita placed a necklace of pearls around his neck. "Hanuman, you are a dear friend. Henceforth you will be known as a champion of the weak and those in trouble." The monkey smiled shyly back at the beautiful princess.

Touching down in his homeland, Rama was crowned King of Ayodhya. He ruled for a very long time with Hanuman by his side.

Valmiki & the Wisdom of Rama

Years passed and, as the great god Shiva promised, Hanuman's fame spread to the four corners of the world.

He also lived longer than everyone else, just as the great god Brahma had said he would. He saw Rama reign gloriously over Ayodhya for many years. When his friends Lakshmana, Sugriva, and Jambavan had all gone, he decided that it was time to retire to the Himalayas. There he lived as a hermit, recounting the honour and glory of the noble Rama of Ayodhya to all who would listen.

One day, as he was wandering on a mountain path, a fierce stranger armed with a dagger accosted him. "Halt!" cried the stranger. "If you resist, I will kill you."

Taken aback, Hanuman stopped in his tracks. "Who are you and what do you want?" he asked.

"I am Valmiki, the *daku.** I rob everyone who comes along this pathway and kill those who resist me. Now, hand over all your belongings."

"Alas," said Hanuman, "I am a hermit and own nothing of value."

"You must have something," insisted the daku.

* *daku.* a robber

"Indeed, I do," replied Hanuman thoughtfully. "I have a story. Would you like to hear it?"

"I suppose it will have to do," said Valmiki reluctantly.

"But before I begin I would like to ask you something," said Hanuman. "Tell me, why do you rob and kill people?"

"I have a wife and several children to support," replied Valmiki. "I am merely doing my parental duty."

"Do you share everything with your family?" asked Hanuman.

"Of course," insisted the daku. "We love each other and share all our joys and sorrows."

"But you will be beheaded if the king's men catch you. Will your family share your death too?" posed Hanuman slyly.

The daku reflected on this question. Finally he replied uncertainly, "I ... I'm not sure."

"Why don't you go and ask them," suggested Hanuman. "I'll wait here until you return."

Valmiki set off to ask his family if they would share his punishment if he were caught, while Hanuman sat patiently by the path.

When the daku reappeared his fierceness was gone. Instead he looked subdued and disappointed.

"Well?" inquired Hanuman, raising an eyebrow.

"Although they are willing to share my spoils, they will not share responsibility for my bad deeds. No one can."

"That is what I thought," said Hanuman. "For you see, Valmiki, no one else can be held responsible for our actions. Now, listen to my story ...

"Long, long ago," he began, "in a city called Ayodhya, there lived a king who had four noble sons. Of them all, the eldest, who was called Rama, was particularly gifted with beauty, strength, and a strong sense of honour ... "

Hanuman then recounted the story of how the noble Prince Rama gave up his throne to honour his father's wishes, and of Sita's rescue. He also spoke of the five sacred principles that Rama had taught him.

"No matter what the provocation," explained Hanuman, "always follow the path of non-violence and truth. There is no other way to lasting peace."

Valmiki's eyes filled with tears as he listened to Hanuman.

"I have done many bad things," he whispered sadly.

"It is never too late to change," encouraged Hanuman.

Valmiki vowed to change his behaviour. "Hereafter I will live according to the code of non-violence and justice."

So saying, he withdrew to the forest to meditate and make amends for his past misdeeds.

Years passed and one day Hanuman found himself wandering the same mountain path where he had met the daku, Valmiki. This time, though, he saw a sage sitting under a tree by the wayside. Dressed in ochre robes, the sage had a snow-white beard and wore his long hair in a knot on top of his head. Around him sat a group of people listening raptly to what he was saying.

"Long, long ago," the sage was saying, "in a city called Ayodhya, there lived a king who had four noble sons. But of them all, the eldest, who was called Rama, was particularly gifted with beauty, strength, and a strong sense of honour ... "

Hanuman smiled happily, for he realized that the sage was none other than Valmiki, the daku. Taking Hanuman's advice to heart, he had given up his wicked ways and become a great sage who was now spreading the teachings of non-violence.

"My mission is over and the time has come for me to join my friends in the afterlife," declared Hanuman. "But a part of me will always linger wherever the story of my dear prince is told."